PRAISE FOR

"A thoughtful treatise to guide a person through difficult but important decisions in preparation for when they are no longer present. You will feel as if Dr. Segal is holding your hand through the process and guides you step-by-step, and thus you will feel her warmth and compassion through it all. A must-have for anyone nearing this time of their life journey."
Monika S. Eichler, LCSW, MEd., CHt

"This instructional manual is a useful tool for anyone. Terry writes about a difficult subject with warmth and compassion, by adding personal anecdotes and notes to her own family."
Sharon Levine Khoury, MSW, ACSW

"A loving thing to do before you pass described by the most loving person I know. Dr. Terry Segal's, *In Loving Memory*, guides you through the creation of a document everyone should consider leaving for their loved ones."
Paul A. Bussard, Author of *Stinger Stars*

"*In Loving Memory* is a concise and informative guide written in Dr. Segal's humorous and loving style. She brilliantly conveys wishes for her family, and assists them in navigating life after death. A must-read for all of us over 50."
Cathy Askowitz Tesserot, Retired Medical Administrator.

"This is a little gem of a book. It offers up reflections on life and what lies beyond. It delves into how to let your loved ones know the ways in which you'd like to

be remembered after your final journey. Despite the heavy-duty nature of the subject matter, Terry Segal's prose is light and lively. A wonderful read."
H. W. "Buzz" Bernard, Author of the award-winning *When Heroes Flew* series.

"I started reading and could not put it down until I finished. I learned. I laughed. I cried. When it comes to the end of life, a Will is financial, but this book is for everything spiritual, physical, emotional, mental, and more."
Jordan Segal, Entrepreneur and Restaurant Owner

"Dr. Terry Segal injects love, humor, and insight into this inspiring guide. She has given us each a gift to be able to choose the way in which we are remembered. As her daughter, I find peace in knowing that she will live forever in our hearts, traditions and celebrations set forth in her own set of instructions. I find comfort in knowing that my children, my children's children, and beyond, will feel connected to this legacy of love. It will inform the way they live."
Sage Segal, Educator and Mother

"I highly recommend this book, and not just because my mom is the author. It's an easy read, and gets the dialogue started on a topic that most people try to avoid. (That's me. I'm most people.) By sitting down with your loved ones and this book, ahead of time, you'll create ways to leave your legacy while making wonderful memories that will live on forever."
Sascha Segal, Accounting Manager and Mother

In Loving Memory

Instructions for Living Without Me

Copyright © 2024 by Terry Segal, Ph.D., all rights reserved. No part of this book may be transmitted, stored, copied or reproduced in any manner or by any means without written permission from Dr. Segal and/or ThomasMax Publishing. An exception will be granted for brief excerpts taken for review purposes.

ISBN-13: 978-1-7377620-9-6
ISBN-10: 1-7377620-9-9

Photo of Dr. Segal by Nicole Tyler
Front cover design by Sage Segal

Published by:

ThomasMax Publishing
P.O. Box 250054
Atlanta, GA 30325

In Loving Memory
Instructions for Living Without Me

By Terry Segal, Ph.D.

ThomasMax Publishing
Atlanta, GA

ABOUT THE AUTHOR

Terry Segal graduated Summa cum laude with a Ph.D. in Energy Medicine from Greenwich University, Australia, while attending a sister University in the United States. She holds a Master of Arts in Educational Psychology from California State University at Northridge, as well as a Master of Arts Degree in Theatre from the University of Miami, in Florida.

She's a licensed Marriage and Family Therapist and Board-Certified Hypnotherapist. She specializes in Energy Medicine and Past-Life Regression Hypnotherapy. Her skills also include Energy Anatomy, Hypnotherapy for Stress Reduction and utilizing the arts as tools for assessment and healing.

Dr. Segal is the author of the non-fiction self-help book, **The Enchanted Journey: Finding the Key That Unlocks You,** and the contemporary women's fiction novel, **Hidden Corners of My Heart.** Her poetry and prose have been published in anthologies: **A Treasure Trove: A Collection of Prose and Poetry, North Point of View: Tales of Alpharetta and Beyond,** and two volumes of **O, Georgia! A Collection of Georgia's Newest and Most Promising Writers.** For more than ten years, she wrote a monthly column, **New Moon Meditations**, for the Atlanta Jewish Times and continues to write articles for them on various topics.

Additionally, she is a union actress and mixed-media artist. Her art has been included in several gallery shows and she has created commissioned pieces of Judaic art for synagogues both in the United States and Israel.

Dr. Segal received the Woman of Achievement Award from The Greater Atlanta Jewish Federation.

This book is dedicated to my family, in past, present and future generations, my friends, clients, and strangers whom, I hope, will honor themselves and support their loved ones by sharing their own personalized instructions before the final breath.

Poem For my grandmother Celia

There are dark and lonely caverns
In the corners of my heart
That once were filled with life, and you,
'Til G-d said we must part.

I used to kiss your petaled cheek
And see you smile at me.
Now the only time that we two meet
Is in loving memory.

FOREWORD

It is an honor to compose this foreword for Dr. Terry Segal's cutting- edge book, *In Loving Memory: Instructions for Living Without Me*. She is a dear friend, colleague, insightful, mindful, and deeply creative, connected soul.

There are many books that give basic steps to laying out the financial aspects of a Will, but there have been none, that I am aware of, that invite you on an inner journey to pause and consider yourself, your heirs, and loved ones, by mindfully sifting through beliefs, emotions and feelings associated with sharing your legacy.

In a hurried world, where ritual is often set aside for the stark contrast of artificial constructs, people have lost sight of the importance of interactions that shape our lives. *In Loving Memory,* kindles exploration, reconciliation, and release of limiting beliefs that create the larger story of your life.

Dr. Segal brings the reader forward, with great care, by weaving intimately and seamlessly, her personal story and her professional acumen of deeply understanding her clients, honed into focus as a therapist for nearly forty years.

In a time where technology is replacing hugs, communication is flattened through emails or text, and the wisdom of the elders is not so readily available, Dr. Segal serves as a loving guide to assist with your living legacy transfer from one generation to the next.

In Loving Memory provides wisdom-infused soil in which to cultivate a protective, loving, even playful mantle of knowledge, traditions, and cherished exchanges for your descendants and loved ones to cherish.

This book is essential for now and for generations to come. It offers practical and creative new concepts to shepherd those who remain after you pass, and encourages new ways to bolster their hearts and enhance their lives.

Immerse yourself in the pages of *In Loving Memory,* and you just might be renewed, inspired, internally transformed, and externally excited, to set about designing your legacy. Let the fresh new concepts in this book enrich the next compelling chapters of your life, and the lives of your loved ones, by providing an integrated map with deep meaning for that day when they will be living without you.

In Loving Memory is an invaluable tool, a must-read on many levels.

Dr. Susan Russell Ph.D.IEM,Th.D Holism L.Ac.,Dipl.Ac., LMSW

CONTENTS

INTRODUCTION: HOW TO LEAVE YOUR OWN INSTRUCTIONS | pg 1

CHAPTER ONE: BEGINNING THE PROCESS | pg 5

CHAPTER TWO: WHEN MY FATHER DIED | pg 9

CHAPTER THREE: YOUR BELIEFS AND WISHES | pg 16

CHAPTER FOUR: THE FIRST YEAR AFTER | pg 19

CHAPTER FIVE: HOW YOU'D LIKE TO BE REMEMBERED | pg 26

CHAPTER SIX: WHEN WISHES CANNOT BE FULFILLED | pg 28

CHAPTER SEVEN: TO A SPOUSE/LIFE PARTNER | pg 33

CHAPTER EIGHT: CONVERSATIONS TO HAVE IN ADVANCE | pg 37

CHAPTER NINE: WINKS AND VISITATIONS FROM THE OTHER SIDE | pg 40

CHAPTER TEN: TO YOUR CHILDREN| pg 55

CHAPTER ELEVEN: YOUR LEGACY STATEMENT | pg 59

CHAPTER TWELVE: YOUR WORLDLY POSSESSIONS | pg 65

CHAPTER THIRTEEN: FINAL THOUGHTS | pg 74

ACKNOWLEDGEMENTS | pg 76

INTRODUCTION: HOW TO LEAVE YOUR OWN INSTRUCTIONS

Most of us would prefer to do anything other than spend time pondering the thought that, one day, we will exit this life. But for those left behind, whether spouses, children, extended family, friends, or even pets, leaving clear directives about what you would want them to do or know, is a gift.

Beyond the details that a legal, written, Last Will & Testament may include, regarding the dissemination of property, valuables and assets, these Instructions also confirm beliefs and offer wishes you may have. You might make suggestions for how your loved ones can honor your birthday each year and what traditions are important to you for the holidays that you'd want passed down through the generations. You could even add to your packet, special recipes, photos, poetry, your signature perfume or cologne, or even articles of clothing. You might choose to release loved ones from debts or grievances that had not been resolved so that you both may be free.

Make changes or additions as you wish. Be sure your loved ones have the contact information for the attorney who has the Will. Make it a priority to draw up a Will if you don't already have one. Many people keep the original and most updated copy in a safe or in the refrigerator, in case of fire or flood. Put a copy of your Instructions with that.

Think of these Instructions like you would the

spare tire in your car. You can check on it to be sure it's there and in good condition but then you don't have to think about it. You hope you never have to use the spare tire but, in the case of these Instructions, it will be used at some point and so helpful to those who may be stranded without you.

Naturally, emotions can arise as you consider all of these aspects of your unique life, circumstances, and relationships. That is not only normal, but expected. Let your tears offer a cleansing for your soul and bring you clarity.

Throughout the book, I share excerpts, containing snippets and stories taken from my own Instructions to my loved ones. I do not reveal, here, where I've stashed my grandmother's cameo pin, nor where the emergency $20 bill is hidden. My mother, of blessed memory, used to keep hers in the bouillon cube container among the spices but I don't use bouillon cubes in my kitchen and I spent the $20 (wisely, of course,) long ago.

If you're like most humans, you've already, repeatedly, shared your thoughts and opinions about how others should live, whether you were asked or not! You might think that writing your wishes is unnecessary. But it isn't. These Instructions to others about how to handle your costume jewelry, what to do with your golf clubs and their grief, and what you desire for them as they heal the hole left by your absence, can bring them, and you, great comfort. It's all stated in one place. No quibbling amongst your loved ones when you're gone.

Writing your Instructions might even consciously shift and inform the way you live your life, which I hope is a long, healthy, and happy one. It's important to note that you don't need to be in your Golden Years or in ill health to write your set of Instructions. While it will not be a legal and binding document, you may wish to update it periodically with the appropriate date on which changes were made.

There's also a section for things to consider putting in place while you're still alive and well, from pre-paid funeral arrangements to teaching or learning how to fill the lawnmower with gas or make an omelet.

I suggest you just read through this book to its end. As you read the excerpts included from my own Instructions, you'll notice that some are most relevant, while others won't apply. That's fine. Just keep reading. It will open your mind and direct your thoughts. Then, you can compile a document of your blueprint for how your loved ones can live without you.

Share what you've written with your loved ones. Discuss requests. It doesn't have to be a grave conversation. (Pun intended.) It can have moments of levity and connection.

As a psychotherapist, I have deep respect and compassion for those whose lives have not been the way they imagined or dreamed. If that describes you, you may think it's pointless to state your wishes now, but it's not. It becomes an act of honoring yourself by putting it out to the Universe. I encourage you to write them.

A note on suicidal ideation. In my professional experience, some people in their own grief, contemplate suicide as an attempt to follow their departed loved ones to the other side. Spirit teaches, however, that the path does not lead others to their loved ones if their actions separated their own soul from its body. Much orchestration has gone into the timing of each conception, planetary configurations, soul cluster, and circumstances, so there is apparently a place of learning in which the soul travels, defeating the intended purpose to join the ones for whom they grieve.

Others contemplate suicide as a means to end their pain. I urge those of you precious beings with suicidal ideation to seek help, and keep seeking help until you find what you need to live with peace and even joy. You may think that everyone would be better off without you but that is rarely the case. Even if you can't imagine it, life can turn around in a moment with unexpected possibilities.

I advise you to tap into your pure soul and to be kind in what you leave behind, whether physical possessions or your words. They will matter to the other souls in your human cluster more than you know.

CHAPTER ONE:
BEGINNING THE PROCESS

Begin by imagining that you're addressing your family, friends, or other loved ones together, as if you've gathered the group to stand before you to hear what you'd like to share. The written Instructions get formed this way and you may decide to actually call your loved ones together in person to read it to them.

Some members of your tribe may refuse to attend a meeting to discuss these issues in person. That's okay. It's another important reason to write them. People may not be able to hear everything when their own emotions are welling up inside of them. When it's in writing, it will be a review if you've spoken about it with them. If not, they can read and re-read it as necessary.

Think about your specific perspective about death and whether you see it as a natural part of life or something separate. What are your own religious or spiritual beliefs about what happens to the soul when a person dies? Do you believe in reincarnation or the afterlife, in Heaven or Hell, and if you'll be met by G-d and loved ones who have gone before you?

Consider your thoughts about sending/receiving messages from the other side and if you have received signs or "winks" in your own experience. All of it becomes fertile ground for exploration and can allow for rich conversations with others. It's a time to express *your* beliefs. Others may not agree with your perspectives but it's not about engaging in heated debates, unless you want that. It's a time to be heard and understood. You can include in your Instructions stories that have shaped your beliefs. Your Instructions can fill half a page or become much longer, as mine have.

EXCERPT TO MY FAMILY

I, being of sound mind and body, want you to have my Instructions for how to live when G-d calls me Home, whenever and however that might be. I believe that a sacred contract exists between G-d and my deepest soul but even I am not consciously privy to it. There are general and specific things I want you to know, stories I want to share or remind you of, and suggestions I'd like to make. I wish to be clear about my Instructions for you for after I'm gone, so there's no disagreement among you about what I would want. This is another way to care for you in what I imagine will be the most difficult and challenging time to be without me.

Note: It's customary in Jewish tradition to hyphenate G-d's name because in the teachings of the Torah we are taught not to erase G-d's name. There are seven names for G-d in Hebrew and none of them are spelled as G-d but I choose to err on the side of being mindful and respectful of this. In modern times, when words are not only erased or thrown out but also deleted, I prefer not to do anything that might lead one to deleting G-d.

When I was growing up, discussions about death were never allowed in my family. We were shielded from death and forbidden to attend funerals of loved ones until we were young adults. My dad, of blessed memory, never wanted me to mention the words, "death, dead, died, dying," or any form of the word, much less have a conversation about it.

I remember once, when I was in elementary school, telling a dramatic story about the earth-shattering events of the day, when I mispronounced a word while reading in front of the class. In recreating it at home, I said, "I almost died!" My father furrowed his eyebrows and his crystal blue eyes, iced. I quickly changed the wording as if to break an imagined spell. "I almost fainted," I said, before continuing on with my story. His facial expression relaxed and his breathing deepened. I understood even then, that he could never touch the imagined grief of being separated from me. I believe he was a bit superstitious about speaking words that referenced death, as if it would bring it closer.

We also weren't allowed to have pets. In a rare moment of using the "D" word himself, my dad said, "Because they die." He added that he wouldn't be able to see me so sad.

In Jewish families, such as my own, it was not uncommon to avoid discussions of death. The names of diseases were whispered. If someone mentioned death, inevitably elder family members would turn two fingers back and forth in front of their mouths, saying, "*Kenahora...* Pu-Pu-Pu!" The Pu-Pu-Pu mimicked spitting. It was as if to spit the word out and cancel it, and put protection around it. The word,

"*Kenahora*" is a combination of Yiddish and Hebrew that loosely translates to, "No evil eye." You don't want to summon death by calling its name, (Pu-pu-pu!) nor do you want to mention something good and jinx it. "*Kenahora*... Pu-Pu-Pu" covers the bases.

It's similar to the Christian protection plan of knocking on wood, which was derived from knocking on the cross at the Crucifixion. In ancient pagan cultures, it was believed that spirits and their gods resided in trees. Knocking on the wooden trunks was thought to rouse these spirits to call on their protection or to show gratitude for good fortune. People didn't want it to be compromised by speaking of it.

I discovered that there's also a Jewish version of "knock on wood," that dates back to the 1490s during the Spanish Inquisition. Under the rule of Torquemada, where only people who believed in Christianity were accepted, Jews were being killed. Fleeing for their lives, the temples built from wood allowed for coded knocks that could be used to gain entry into these safe structures. Many lives were saved and "knocking on wood" became associated with good luck.

So, this is your place, no matter your religious or spiritual beliefs, to actually think and speak about death with your loved ones.

CHAPTER TWO: WHEN MY FATHER DIED

As the Universe would have it, in the pre-dawn hours of the day he died, I was the first to have heard him get up to use the bathroom which preceded a huge crash. The mighty oak of my father apparently had a heart attack and had fallen over, head first, into the tub. I, at the age of 22, had literally just completed a CPR class I "randomly" took. Without hesitation, I ran into the bathroom, moved him into position, his dear face bloodied, and began CPR breathing and chest compressions.

Shielded from death for all of those years, I was then first in line to prevent death from entering the room. And I failed, which was something that I wasn't used to doing. Performing CPR had been much easier with Resusci Annie, the training mannequin. I had no deeply loving and abiding relationship with her and was not choked with emotion in class. Given all of this, with my father, I knew that I had performed the life-saving techniques correctly. After several rounds of no movement from him though, I began to breathe harder, faster, and became exhausted and light-headed. I squeezed aside in the tiny bathroom to allow access for my mother, as I instructed her to take over administration of the life-saving techniques that did not save my father's life.

I was devastated when the paramedics arrived and were also unsuccessful at reviving him. They asked me a few questions and provided explanations that comforted me. They determined that because his hands were behind his back when he fell over the tub, he had very likely had the heart attack and died instantly, before the fall, and before I even began the breathing. Otherwise, instinctively, he would have had his hands out front, to break his fall. They confirmed that I had done everything right and that nothing and no one could have revived him. It was his time.

During that week, I had been in final dress rehearsals as an actress for the show, *Cyrano de Bergerac*, at the Coconut Grove Playhouse in Miami, Florida. I had been preparing to do ten shows a week, when I "heard" angelic whisperings that I needed to take a CPR class. It was the end of December, an already busy time of year, but I heeded the "whisperings" to take the course. I knew, without a doubt in the aftershock, that if I had encountered that moment and was unprepared with life-saving knowledge that could have saved his life, I would've never forgiven myself.

The following night Mom and Dad had tickets to the opening which I, of course, missed. Dad's urgency to attend final dress rehearsal suddenly made sense. With all of the shows I'd been in over the years, he and Mom always attended opening night and never the final dress rehearsal. His angels must have whispered to him that he needed to see the show because he'd no longer be here the next night when it opened.

Our family sat *shiva*, ("seven" in Hebrew) which

is the Jewish custom of seven days of mourning. The main purpose is to provide time for the shift into spiritual and emotional healing. The community joins the mourners and makes sure that they are fed and cared for during the transition to life without the presence of the person who has died.

It was January, the first week of the new year. I knew that life would never be the same without him and I couldn't imagine going to the theatre and pretending to be some character who experienced joy and brought that joy and laughter to an audience of strangers. But I heard his voice, as clearly as if he were standing right next to me. He didn't want to hear my name substituted with the young woman playing my role in my absence. He urged me to return to the theatre and so after a week of sitting *shiva,* I did. I performed my role for him at each matinee and every night, for the run of the show, grateful that he had seen it.

EXCERPT TO MY FAMILY

Because of my life-altering experience with my dad's passing, I've always talked to you, my precious children, about all of it, and listened to what you had to say, even when it was tough for me, as this is now. I taught you about life by example each day, through love, my actions, communication, the written words of others and my own, through my life's work as a psychotherapist, and through my art. Each of you has learned different things from me as your individual needs were addressed. I always tried to answer you honestly, with integrity, and in conversations that were age-appropriate for your levels of understanding.

After having worked and lived on two coasts, simultaneously, going back and forth between New York and California when I was modeling, dancing, and acting, I settled in California when I married Daddy. You know that from the time we conceived each of you that family has always been the number one priority in our lives. We've worked hard at our careers but there was never a thought that anything other than family was more important.

We established a foundation for life based on our religious and spiritual beliefs, as well as the wisdom gained from my study of psychology. This has included the teachings of our Jewish traditions, in addition to the metaphysical principles of energy exchange, the presence of angels as G-d's messengers, intentional thought, and healing through the use of herbs and nutrition. Awareness is required in the process of mindful creation of life's enchanted beauty. Reverence for your body as a Holy vessel that houses your precious mind and spirit is vital.

I'm sure that each of you knows what I believe and what I'd do in most situations. Remember to ask yourself what you think I would say or do if it's a time that you need me. Even if you make a different decision, I feel confident that you would know what I'd advise and that I trust your own wisdom. You all have surprised me, many times, with the ways in which you have "heard" me, even when it seemed that you might have not been listening or were too young to comprehend.

I recall the time when we were back in Florida and I was driving, just with Jordan, in the car. Jordan, I know you've heard the story many times, but I want you to remember it and tell it to others. You were four years old, and in your booster carseat, in the back. As I happened to pass Memorial West Hospital in Cooper City, you drew in a gasping breath and released it in racking sobs. I immediately pulled into the hospital parking lot and leapt out of the car and into the back seat. "What's wrong, Sweetheart?" I asked, as I put my arms around you and held you before unbuckling your seatbelt. You were inconsolable, your sweet face flooded with tears. You hugged me tightly and between gasps asked, "What if I die one day and I can't find you in my next lifetime?" This still brings me to my knees...We sat there for quite awhile and talked through it.

I was a California Board-Certified Hypnotherapist who additionally had extensive training in Past-Life Regression Hypnotherapy, but you didn't know that. You'd tell me grand stories that often began with, "Mommy, remember when I was a cook and baker man in New York and remember how so many people lined up for soup and bread and I made it for them?"

Because of my background, I listened with an open mind and heart and could recognize that the details you shared were beyond your current-life experience or knowledge. You'd even advise me when I was baking, and I always listened to you. Within my framework, I believed that a previous-life experience was seeping into and informing this one.

From a young age, you also possessed such precision and skill for technical drawing. That, combined with your desire to be outdoors, had me imagining that you'd become a landscape architect. But by age seven you were also turning out perfect omelets and making French toast. It was no surprise that, at the age of 16, you had drawn up a 60-page proposal of the breakfast/lunch cafe you'd open to feed family, friends, and a whole community of people who could taste the love in the food you'd serve them. We watched with pride and astonishment when, upon graduation from the university's business school, you set about making that dream a reality and opened your first location of your cafe at the age of 24.

I know that you're in a constant state of communication with G-d and gratitude for all you've accomplished. It's important to nourish the dreams and desires of the soul and use your G-d-given gifts to make the world a better place.

It's clear that you draw upon your lifetime as a "cook and baker man" in your daily life, now. I also observe how you mindfully and quickly discern what is in your control to change and what is not, and how you catch and release those things beyond your control, and turn them over to G-d. I watch you assess, make decisions, and take action, moving on from the challenges and disappointments swiftly toward your next step. You have taught me in this process. Just like my dad knew that I understood him, I know that you have heard and understand me, and my beliefs that support yours.

While each of you has heard what we believe and value, in no way does that mean that you have blindly followed what Daddy and I have set out for you. I trust that each soul has a sacred contract with G-d and that each soul has been granted free will. Often, paths are taken that no one understands but they are ones that progress the soul's learning. The impact on the soul cluster of those in the closest part of the circle have learning through these challenges too. The words contained in my Instructions are simple and also complex, because they are an extension of all of that learning we've done together.

At the heart of it all, love is all that matters. If there are differences in the family, work through them. You may disagree on some issues, but love must prevail. I'd never want any of you, my sweet children, to be separate from one another.

CHAPTER THREE:
YOUR BELIEFS AND WISHES

I invite you to write your thoughts to your family, spouse, or life-partner on all of the topics it may have been too difficult to discuss before now. Consider how you can help your loved ones move through their grieving process. Do you have any suggestions for how they might celebrate your birthday that first year without you? How would you like to be remembered? Are there any traditions at specific holidays that you'd like passed down to future generations or celebrated among friends? Are there recipes you need to actually write down for others?

Most of us would not want our loved ones to only remember us with breathless sobs. It's a process. Your loved ones should know that, of course, there are tears and heartache at the void left by your absence. There will also be funny instances and glorious memories that bring smiles and joy. Those two things seem far apart at first, but grief is a journey. Laughter and tears can occur simultaneously. Years later, specific times or events may evoke tears again, but these feelings should not interfere with the ability to live their G-d-given lives.

Encourage them now, while you can, to seek help if they find themselves unable to move on with their lives. Some references will site a 6-month period, but I don't believe that there is an exact time frame. They will know in their hearts if their grief is overwhelming them. Others will become concerned so urge them to listen.

Sometimes, if a person has valiantly battled a disease or has been in unspeakable pain, there is relief that they are no longer suffering. I have sat with people who then feel guilty that they didn't cry and were only relieved to have their loved ones released to peace. If you would want your loved ones to also feel released from the suffering they endured alongside of you, then include that to ease their pain.

EXCERPT TO MY CHILDREN

You know that Daddy always tells me that he wishes for me to throw him off the cliff if he gets demented. That's not going to happen.

As for me, if I get dementia, Pu-Pu-Pu, of course I would like to stay in my home, with in-house care. Knowing the best laid plans and heartbreak of having to put a loved one into a facility after all, I apologize, in advance, if it comes to that. You will have to do what works for everyone in the family. You know that I have done everything on my end to mindfully eat well, exercise, keep my mind sharp, etc. so it would be G-d's will, and my soul's sacred contract, if that occurs. That was, perhaps, the only way I was able to separate from my mother at the end, when it happened to her. Please don't wait too long to get help if I need that level of care. I don't expect any of you to become a nursemaid or caretaker, pushing yourself beyond boundaries that are comfortable or that become unhealthy for you. Please, however, be patient with me as I have been with you.

I'm also requesting that, if possible, you help me to maintain my dignity, especially if I am not able. That's important to me. Also, wearing lipstick, perfume, combing my hair, and maintaining excellent hygiene matter deeply to me. I do not want to smell like Limburger cheese at the end of my life. Please visit me, kiss my cheek, hold my hand, and tell me you love me, but don't compromise your own health in the process.

As for my remains, a pine box with a Star of David on it is all I need. Don't get talked into a Medieval casket with purple velvet lining. Go on vacation with the extra money that would cost. Throw a little glitter in with me and I'll be happy and fancy. As Nanny said of herself, "I'll become compost for the earth." Beautiful trees for you to hug. Please plant trees for me in Israel and wherever else you'd like. I'll be sure to visit and tend to them.

CHAPTER FOUR: THE FIRST YEAR AFTER

That first year is often a difficult adjustment. There's a desire to honor the departed without constantly tearing open the scab of the emotional healing. Suggest to your loved ones how they may maneuver their way through this time. Maybe you always went to special destinations for a vacation or holiday. Give them permission to continue to go there and remember the good times along with making new memories. You might also suggest a new place they can go that you have chosen for them.

They probably already know your favorite holidays, sports teams, foods, etc. but glance through the calendar and acknowledge which ones you suspect may be tough for them and offer some thoughts about it.

For example, I had hand painted several sweatshirts for my own mother that she wore right up until her last days when she was 91. After her passing, on her birthday that first year, our daughters and I wore those sweatshirts and we enjoyed her favorite foods for a birthday dinner in her memory. Mom loved pistachio nuts and pistachio ice cream. Now, every year on her birthday, each of us is sure to eat some pistachio nuts. My mother's favorite perfume was Ciara. I saved her half-full bottle and we've used it for group spritzing on her birthday. We still miss her terribly but have made new memories in her honor.

On Passover, at the Seder, we read from the *Haggadah,* the Jewish text that sets forth the order and fulfills the commandment to tell the story from the Book of Exodus about G-d bringing the Israelites out of slavery in Egypt. Mom's favorite part, that was always hers to read aloud, was about "one little goat, one little goat that I bought for two *zuzim*." The first year without her was so emotional that we all sobbed and read her part together.

At Halloween, Mom used to dress up as a friendly witch to greet Trick or Treaters at her door. I did as well and that first Halloween, Sage, our youngest who was away at college, suggested we display Mom's witch hat and her toy bats and pumpkins on our dinner table. We did.

As for me, I've made it my mission to make all of life as enchanting as possible so there is always something to celebrate! We have created many traditions together that I hope will sustain my family and be passed along through the generations.

EXCERPT TO MY FAMILY

On my birthday, let everyone dress in my favorite shades of purple, have a picnic, and eat organic hotdogs and mint chip ice cream with chocolate cake and berries! Be sure to have a bottle of my signature fragrance, Calvin Klein's Obsession, to dab on everyone. Sascha and Sage, you might want to save and wear special articles of my clothing and jewelry, as we did with Nanny. Actually, more than clothing, wear my aprons. You each have gifted me with such special ones, I'd love for you to keep them, wear them, and even pass them along…latke oil stains and all. For me, eat a square of dark chocolate each year as you relish the memory of the amazing adventures we had in the everyday moments of life.

For each of your birthdays, my greatest joy would be in seeing you happy, loved, and celebrated.

Take time to honor the change of seasons and look ahead to the next three month cycle for your attunement to nature. Blossom in the spring, shine in the summer, reap the fruits of your labor in autumn, and restore and find some stillness in winter. Also sanctify the New Moon. That was the first commandment to our people. Acknowledge Rosh Chodesh (the head of the Hebrew month) which is based upon the lunar calendar.

As I look through both the Hebrew and Gregorian calendars, there are many special opportunities for celebration. You know that a long time ago, I made the legacy recipe book, A Taste of Home, with all of our favorite recipes and the holidays on which I made them. Please continue to add to it and taste the love in every dish.

Party decorations can consist of favorite photos of us, together or, more likely, ones that I photographed. These can be swapped out on Valentine's Day, Mother's Day, Purim, Halloween and Chanukah. If you don't do any of this, I won't be mad. I'd only be upset if you let the darkness of grief cloud the beauty of each G-d-given day and overshadow the blessed memories we've all created together.

Valentine's Day might be especially tough, but remember that it's a day of love and I've always been all about that. However you do love, do it up on this day.

You know that every year we would have our Valentine's Day card making and pizza party! We had so much fun. If you continue this tradition, make a card for yourself from me. I will love you always and forever.

I would ask that you host or attend a Seder each year on Passover. Of course you know that my special part of the Seder has been the acting out of the Ten Plagues. There's a box in the basement storage area labeled PASSOVER. In advance, be sure that there are representations of each of the ten plagues, especially the boils. That must be checked a few days prior, in case you need to make more. Paint Band-aids with red, yellow, and green acrylic paint or puffy paint in those colors and let it dry. Each of you already knows how to turn the water into "blood." Sascha, I know that you were 34 years old when you figured this out so I'm not ruining anything here by telling you. Have two clear pitchers. Carefully place the drops of red food coloring in a circle around the bottom inside edge of one pitcher and hold that one up briefly so everyone can see that it's empty. Fill the second pitcher with water, and highlight that one. Little ones can inspect the water pitcher and should be amazed when you pour the water one into the "empty" other pitcher with the food coloring in it and it splashes up red. Tell all of those present that the One Little Goat part is forever in honor of Nanny.

Mother's Day may be bittersweet but be sure your children celebrate you! This might be a good moment to share legacy wishes or beliefs I've handed down to you that you'd like to hand down to yours. Jordan, since you're not a mother, please continue to celebrate your sisters as mothers and share the stories with all of the children in the family, too. It has truly been my greatest honor and privilege to be the mother of the three of you.

I know on Father's Day and Daddy's birthday you will joyfully celebrate him and also support him each and every day in my absence.

It's important to me that you continue to observe the Holy Days of Rosh Hashanah (the Jewish New Year) and Yom Kippur (the Day of Atonement.) It is often difficult to go against the mainstream flow and say that your children won't play sports or attend school on those days but it is my wish that you will immerse yourself in the meaning and ritual of these days in some way that connects you to G-d and sustains our traditions.

Halloween should just be fun! You'll have the recipe in that book for making the garlic witches' fingers and toes with the green pistachio nut nails. Also in there are the instructions for filling the punch bowl with cranberry juice and floating the ice hand in it. Just remember before you freeze the water in a latex glove, to rinse it out first, because they put powder in them to make them easier to wear.

Thanksgiving and Chanukah may also be among the more difficult times. For Thanksgiving, again, the recipes are all there. The most important ingredient in every dish is love, so put a lot into each dish. There is no such thing as too much.

For Chanukah, and all gift-giving holidays, you know that I like reusable gift bags for the environment, so there isn't so much wasted gift wrap. All of you remember how Nanny would take the tissue paper inside of the bags and lovingly fold and smooth them out to be reused. Well, you can stack them and with an iron on the lowest heat setting, press them to be reused and crisp for many celebrations to come.

Saying the Mourner's Kaddish for my parents every night for the eleven months after their deaths became very grounding for me. I felt joined with those who went before and recited the same prayers for their departed ones. It actually felt odd for me to stop reciting it nightly when it was complete. Both Daddy and I would ask that you recite the prayer in the customary way for us.

Note: The Mourner's Kaddish is a very important Jewish ritual recited on behalf of the deceased, praising G-d. In fact, (like my father's teachings) nowhere in this prayer is there a reference to death or dying, only praise to G-d. Death can test faith and this prayer grounds us in G-d's greatness.

The prayer is to be recited, daily, for 11 months from the date of passing for a parent, and for 30-days for other loved ones.

Our wise sages teach that "Every Jewish person reveals a particular expression of G-dliness in this world. Once he or she passes away, G-d's radiance is 'diminished' somewhat in this world. When Kaddish is recited, it restores this radiance and brings additional glory to G-d's name in this world."

In Jewish mysticism, there are ten words of praise included in Kaddish that correlate to the ten *Sefirot* or Divine manifestations. These are related to the ten Utterances of Creation, which suggests that those who are living have a role in perfecting Creation.

CHAPTER FIVE:
HOW YOU'D LIKE TO BE REMEMBERED

Think about how you'd like to be remembered for your time on this good earth. Would it be for qualities you possess, a special talent, or your amazing barbeque sauce? Maybe you'd like different groups of people in your life to remember different things about you. You may wish for your family to remember you as the breadwinner who kept food on the table or the parent who kissed the boo-boos and made them better. Perhaps you'd like your co-workers to remember you as a passionate leader or as someone who never backed down in the face of adversity. You may hope that your Mahjong friends will treasure the memory of how you made them laugh. Think about your impact on others, both positive and negative. While there's still time, maybe express regret for the negatives and release them, while building upon the positives.

EXCERPT TO MY FAMILY

It would be my honor to be remembered as some-one who sought enchantment in the mundane, loved deeply, and brought happiness, comfort, compassion, and healing to others. How lucky I am to have experienced the deepest love in choosing my best friend to marry and, with whom I have created this loving family of ours. I am forever grateful that each of you has expressed, daily, the depth of your exquisite love for me. It brings me to tears of profound gratitude.

In the Jewish community, I can only hope that I was seen as a Woman of Valor, worthy of that title. I hope that my art and writing that honors the *Shekinah,* the Divine Feminine, remains a source of the reverence I have for the Sisterhood of our people and all people.

To my friends, near and far, I have tried to always be present for you, in good times and bad. We didn't travel as much as I wished we could have and I hope that you understand.

It is my deepest hope that my clients know their sacred and special place in my heart. I've been honored to walk with them on their journey toward healing and wholeness, in the direction of living a life that is filled with Divine sparks of enchantment in each day. I hope they will hear my voice in the dark times, comforting and guiding them, and remember that the angels are ever-present and that they are never alone.

I realize that someone in the family will be charged with the task of making the difficult phone calls to others with the sad news. I also know that the younger ones prefer not to talk on the phone and would rather send a group communication through technology but, if at all possible, verbal communication would be preferred, at least for the closest of family, friends, and my clients. As always, know my wish but do what you are able to do.

CHAPTER SIX:
WHEN WISHES CANNOT BE FULFILLED

I'm including this because there are times when others cannot fulfill the wishes of their loved ones. Your Instructions, as I've said, should serve as a guideline rather than a demand that can leave a loved one feeling inept, or worse, that they've disappointed you once you're gone.

When my dear mother was in the throes of her increasing dementia, she also had moments/days of great clarity. Throughout both of those times she was clear that, when the day came, she wanted to die in her home, not a facility. She tried to make me promise that. I promised that I would do all that was humanly possible to fulfill her wishes, but added that if she became a danger to herself or others, I would need to take another course of action. I told her that I hoped she could know and accept, somewhere inside of herself, that I was doing the right thing.

During one painful conversation, after several falls in her home and in public, followed by many trips to the ER, she told me point blank, that if she fell off her deck, hit her head and bled to death, there would be no better place for her to die than in her garden. She said she could become compost for her flowers and that if I found her there, I should just let it play out. I could not agree to that. For the first time in my life with her, I felt her anger and disappointment in me. That cut through me like a knife.

After a few days of unrestrained tears, I called the

man who was my rabbi at the time. I told him of my personal dilemma regarding the commandment to Honor Thy Father and Thy Mother. I asked him how I could honor my mother's wishes when they flew in the face of her safety and wellbeing. I shared that I also could not participate in the request to do nothing to save her.

He said that preserving her life takes precedent over all and spoke of *pikuach nefesh*. It's an obligation for all Jews, he explained, in which we have a duty to save a person's life if we can, even if doing so means that another *mitzvah* (commandment) will be broken. For example, a doctor can break the Sabbath to save a person's life, and food that is not kosher can be eaten in order to survive. It is derived from the biblical verse, "Neither shall you stand by the blood of your neighbor," (Lev. 19:16), which, in this case, was my mother. He said that even though it seemed like I'd be honoring her by acting on her wishes, saving her life was above that. He talked about doing the right thing as she would wish if she were in her right mind. His words brought me great peace.

Over the course of the next several months, Mom continued to outsmart home health-care providers with her strong will and creative plans. She had, however, become a danger to herself and others, in terms of almost burning the house down when she went to bake cookies and, instead of turning on the upper oven, heated the lower one, which housed all of her Tupperware. It was one of many ways in which she was unsafe and it was heart-breaking.

On another occasion, I had taken her to Wal-Mart, at her request, and suddenly could see that she was about to faint. I couldn't hold her up and so I put my arms around her from behind and rolled down on to my back on the ground as she collapsed on top of me. Thankfully many people rushed to help. The manager called 9-1-1 and the paramedics allowed me to ride in the ambulance with her. She came to and was upset to find herself on the way to the hospital. I calmed her. Again, once we arrived at the hospital and she was placed in an examination room, she coded. The team rushed in to perform heroic, life-saving measures that included cutting her new blouse in two. They had paddles on her and I stood in the corner of the room, Archangel Michael's wings holding me vertical, as I watched from out of my body, praying and reviewing each of my decisions. When the episode was over and she returned to full consciousness, she was *"pissed off"* that I had let them cut her new shirt. But I knew it was the right thing. She moved past it and a few days later when I drove her home, she thanked me for taking such good care of her.

And so it went for a year and a half when, exhausted, we were in the process of needing to place my mother in a facility. The situation had become unmanageable and I fully realized it when the staff at the ER knew me by name and talked to me about that.

It was one of the hardest things I've ever done. I repeated the rabbi's words to myself throughout the entire process and felt completely sure of my actions all throughout the rest of her life.

Unlike the example of my own upbringing, I had "forced" a few conversations a decade earlier, when we had taken Mom to the attorney's office to draw up a Will and, then again, when I knew that I had done all I could to keep her safe in her home.

There had been many, many incidents leading up to that before I reached out for help and I realized, well after the fact that, to my own detriment, I had waited too long to get help. In hindsight, I put her desires ahead of my own wisdom for much longer than I should have, in an attempt to fulfill her wishes. That's a motivating factor in writing my own Instructions. I want my wishes to be clear, right along with my understanding that they may not unfold the way I envision them. I offer love and forgiveness, in advance, to my loved ones who may have to make some tough choices. I encourage you to be clear with your loved ones as well and offer forgiveness, if possible, in advance.

Speaking of wishes that can't be fulfilled…I've tried having these conversations with my husband. He vacillates between tears and a dark sense of humor. He said to me that if he loses his faculties, I should just throw him off a cliff. First of all, we don't live in a place that has cliffs and, more importantly, I told him that I don't wish to live out my Golden Years in jail due to honoring his Instructions.

From time to time he will walk into the room and start a conversation with, "You know I'm claustrophobic and even though I would already be dead, I'd suffocate in a casket." Okay! He liked my inane suggestion that I could perhaps put a PVC pipe in the ground next to the casket so he'd have an air hole. It was better than the one he came up with two weeks later, to let them lower him in the casket but not close it or cover it over with dirt because he would hate that.

You might be thinking that cremation would be the answer but, in case you're not familiar with Jewish customs, cremation is not a traditional choice. There are prohibitions on defiling a dead body, which is considered to be the property of G-d, and there are detailed procedures about how to handle the body prior to burial. They all go against the act of cremation. The Jewish mystics believed that the soul does not immediately separate from the body upon death and that decay into the earth allows for a more gradual separation.

Practicality, expense, and more modern beliefs make allowances for this choice in some instances. If you, in your choices, wish to be cremated, be sure that your desires are known.

Meanwhile, even though my husband continues to offer macabre suggestions, I do know his wishes are to have a simple, pine box with a Star of David on it, and to be sent off on words of love and gratitude for being granted such a special and enchanted life.

CHAPTER SEVEN:
TO A SPOUSE/LIFE PARTNER

What would you like your spouse/life partner to know? Share your thoughts about them falling in love again or finding a new partner. Some people say, "I don't care. When I'm dead, I'm dead." Others might make statements that could potentially leave a partner riddled with guilt for thoughts about moving on with their lives. I remind you to be honest but kind in your Instructions. Your wishes are important but they should not be intended to rule the lives of those left behind.

EXCERPT TO MY HUSBAND

To my dear Sweetheart and best friend. I'm drowning in a river of tears as I write this to you. I have loved you from the moment I met you, I love you still, and will love you from across the worlds, always and forever.

I know that you and I have tried to have discussions about this, in the darkness of night, when the kids were small and in their beds, and also when they were grown and tucking their own little ones in for the night. We never got very far. We both ended up sobbing and holding each other, too distraught at the thought of being separated. But if I look at this as the gift that I believe it is, I can continue writing it to completion.

We have a lifetime of reading each other's thoughts, finishing each other's sentences, and working hard to make each other laugh, whenever possible and appropriate. Also, at those times when it wasn't necessarily appropriate. Like at the theatre in California with the Billy Barty incident or at the George Wallace comedy show when I was laughing so hard I could not rein myself in. You remember…Please also remember the sound of my laughter. I will forever remember yours.

Although you'll be grieving, please stay hydrated and eat, even if you don't want to. Cry whenever you need to but be sure to also laugh, as that will help keep you healthy. Remember to live in the "and," not the "either/or." Most people feel like they have to either be sad and grieving or happy. I think it's best when we can live in the "and." For example, "I feel very sad right now AND I can watch a show that makes me laugh." Conversely, "I am enjoying this moment at the concert AND I feel sad at not having you here with me." Don't feel guilty for smiling, laughing, or having a good time. I promise it's what I want for you and the family as well. Please talk about the good times and pass the stories down. Talk to me out loud if you wish. I promise to try and hear you and respond.

Please continue to look after the wellbeing of our children and grandchildren (and hopefully great grandchildren by then!) People can hide their emotions and/or suffering so listen to everything they're saying and also what they're not saying. You know from living with me all of these years, as the husband of a therapist, what that means.

I'd like to ask you, if I go first, to wait at least one year after my passing before you entertain the thought of engagement or marriage to another woman. I've already promised that I won't haunt you. I know that we've said that we're like lobsters, mating for life, but in my research, I discovered that this reference from the TV show, F.R.I.E.N.D.S., was inaccurate. Lobsters actually not only don't mate for life but the male has a harem of female lobsters! It turns out that only certain animals mate for life: Among them are Beavers, Seahorses, Macaroni Penguins, Barn Owls, Bald Eagles, Gibbons, and Wolves. I know, as the eternal student, I'm still learning things and sharing them with you.

I digress.

The takeaway here is that they mate for life. Nothing is mentioned beyond that. It's important, in my personal and professional opinion, to experience that first year after a loved one's passing, to move through those "firsts," without them, as part of the grieving process and not try to bypass them. Please, however, even during that time, continue to laugh and grow and make memories beyond me.

If you never want to date or remarry, I would understand because I can't imagine ever doing that if the situation were reversed. Humans are designed not to be alone, however, and only my earthly personality wouldn't want to share you. My Higher Self would not want you to walk this life alone. Thank G-d we have a close-knit, loving family so you won't be alone, but companionship is different.

You know I like to be in control of things so I would try to choose someone for you from my reserved spot, hopefully in Heaven, but I think it would be tough for our kids to see her living in our house, cooking in my kitchen, planting in my garden, and sleeping in our bed, so you might have to consider moving. I know that there are so many memories in every crack and floorboard of our home. Our love is so special that I don't want it to die when one of us does, but I also don't want to be a ghost that interferes with your future. I want the best for you, always.

I can't imagine that another woman could feel at home in our home, anyway. It's infused with our love. Hopefully, our home can go to a family member in that case but if not, bless it and all that took place in it and begin the next chapter of your beautiful life. Please know that I want what you would want for yourself.

If you decide to stay in our home, please let the love envelope you and only serve as a source of joyful memory.

CHAPTER EIGHT:
CONVERSATIONS TO HAVE IN ADVANCE

We all get into habits and routines in life and assume we aren't going to keel over suddenly and die. But that happens all of the time, every day, somewhere, leaving most loved ones unprepared to cope with the responsibilities left for them to handle.

Think about what responsibilities you are in charge of that would be helpful for others to have listed for them. Where is your Last Will & Testament? Have you updated it? Where is the important banking information, computer passwords, and contact information for all doctors, attorneys, friends and family members? Where is the deed to the house? What do you need to teach someone how to do and, conversely, what might you need to learn? Make a list. Emotions can get in the way of your thoughts and you won't remember any of this if you don't write it down.

SEEK LEGAL ADVICE

As we age, most of us don't envision ourselves living in a nursing home during the last chapter of our lives. We assume we will be healthy until our final moments or will have family care for us or hire caregivers in our home. We often think of our home as the place where we will live and die.

If you don't want to live in a nursing home, there are some things you can do in advance to prepare.
. These helpful tips about advance planning come

from the Hurley Elder Care Law Office, with whom I have taken CEUs (Continuing Education Units) for my psychotherapy license. I, however, have no affiliation with them beyond that. You can check your local advisors for information in your area.

The Hurley Law Office suggests a strategy for building a **team of experts**, such as an experienced CPA, financial advisor and an elder law attorney to stretch your money. **Trust planning** is also suggested, as is looking into all **available benefits** due you, such as Medicaid or Veteran's Administration programs. (Many of these take significant time to implement and so beginning well in advance of needing them is advised.) **Talking to your family** is also on their to-do list of important matters. They offer information about help for those who are **living alone,** through their Aging Ally services. It addresses concerns of those who don't have a support network, who are afraid that an ailing spouse will outlive them, and how to make decisions regarding **future care** and who will make decisions if the person living alone is incapacitated and in an emergency situation. These are all vital discussions to have in advance because the process of planning for care can feel overwhelming.

EXCERPT TO MY HUSBAND

I hope you're looking this over before my time with you has ended because I have some questions. You know that with our division of labor, you've handled all of the black and white, nuts and bolts of life. You've always been "the black and white to my lavender." You've been in charge of the financial matters, warranties, vehicles, and the remote for the TV. I probably wouldn't be able to turn the thing on without you.

On the other hand, I have been the head chef, grill mistress, decorator, organizer, planner, gardener, mother, grandmother, and enchantment specialist. Still, I'd be lost without you. This applies to my wandering in the cavernous space that would house the fragmented shards of my heart and also, being clueless as to what all of the bills are and where and when they get paid. When I was single, 150 years ago, I handled all of these things myself but it has been a long time and the world has changed. You know I've just deposited my earnings in our account and you did the rest.

I've always spoken about the importance of each person knowing everything that constitutes running the household but I have been remiss. I've been too busy with my lavender responsibilities to focus on the black and white constants. In this moment it feels less important to teach you about changing the nature table each season or how the prop closet is organized by seasons to set all of the tablescapes, and more important to find out about the light bill so I'm not in the dark. Please make a list of everything, sit me down, and fill me in. I might resist. Okay, yes, I will resist. Also, include this in your list of Instructions to others.

CHAPTER NINE: WINKS AND VISITATIONS FROM THE OTHER SIDE

Whether or not you believe that loved ones can connect from the other side, take a moment to recall if you've experienced "G-d winks," Divine interventions, messages, or even visitations from those who have departed, that cannot be explained any other way.

To me, an example of a Divine intervention occurred one night, many years ago, in which my husband and I were in the car on the way home. It was dark and he was driving. We had been stopped at a red light and when it turned green, he didn't go. I asked why he wasn't moving and he said he didn't know. Seconds later, a drunk driver raced through the red light at a high speed, right where our car would have been making the turn if we had gone when the light changed. It was a deeply sacred moment.

I believe in synchronistic occurrences and don't view them as "coincidence." I also believe that souls of our beloved ones can, if granted permission from the Divine hierarchy, communicate with us.

I've also sat with clients who have been afraid that those departed ones who caused them harm now have a voyeuristic view of their lives. There does not seem to be any subjective evidence of that. Through anecdotal accounts, it appears to be something granted, as not to interfere with the lives of the living, in limited ways, to souls who have evolved through learning.

I have witnessed contact made, on many occasions, during sessions with clients. In one instance, a client who has granted me permission to share her story, was anguishing over her decision about whether or not to marry the man who had just proposed to her. While she was talking, I had an overwhelming sensory experience of the fragrance of a rose garden. I dismissed it at first and continued listening to my client's reasoning. She said, "I wish I knew what to do." The fragrance became so strong that I felt moved to mention it. I told her that this may sound crazy, but that I was either having an olfactory hallucination or someone was trying to make contact. I said that there was a very strong and beautiful fragrance of roses, as if standing in a garden of them. I wondered aloud if this had any meaning for her. She burst into tears and said that it had to be her departed grandmother, whose name was Rose.

This was not the first time for me that a specific rose fragrance was detected and that a relative named Rose was making contact. When this particular Rose was young, the client told me that a rose bush had been planted each year on her birthday. As an adult, she planted a huge rose garden of her own and from the time my client was very young, until her grandmother's death, they would walk and talk in the garden. I asked her how she thought her Grandma Rose would advise her about the young man to whom she was engaged and if she'd be in favor of them getting married.

My client immediately said, "No!" She began

talking about all of the qualities of a husband that her grandmother used to talk to her about and her fiancé did not possess them. He was good to her most of the time but had an awful temper and mistreated her at other times. We had been exploring that in depth but she kept getting drawn back into the relationship by him. During one of his apology phases, he proposed. Realizing that her grandmother was unwavering about those kinds of behaviors, my client immediately felt clear and decided to break off their engagement. I believe that it was nothing short of contact from the other side of the veil.

Author Jenny Heston describes the veil as such: "You might say the veil is the place where the everyday illusion of separation brushes up against the divine truth of eternity and universal interconnection. The place where form meets spirit, seen meets unseen, known meets unknown."

VISITS FROM MY DAD

I've always known that neither my mother nor father would visit in a way that would scare me. I've had several palpable visits from my dad. I cherish the memory of them. One occurred in a dream. I heard him call my name and I turned in his direction. Everything looked foggy but he stepped forward and I saw him. Running to him, I thought, *I haven't seen him for so long!* But in the dream I didn't remember that he had died. We threw our arms around each other and he hugged me as he had when I was little. The rush of safety and security permeated my body.

It reminded me of how I felt when I was very young and used to stand on his feet while he danced with me. Then, when I was too sleepy, he'd pick me up and I'd lie my head down on his shoulder and close my eyes while he carried me to my bed and gently placed me in it. He'd kiss me on the forehead and whisper, "Goodnight, sweet dreams," before walking out of my room. I wanted to stay in that embrace but, in the dream, his body became less dense. He got lighter and lighter until I could see through him and then suddenly, he disappeared into the foggy air and I was standing alone. I wept, being without him again, but after I fully awakened, knew that somehow he was granted a visit and crossed back over from the other side to hug me.

Another "visitation" from my Dad occurred after my own family, along with my mother, were in the 1994 Northridge, California, earthquake. Following several days of severe aftershocks, we called a moving company, contacted our family and friends, had four hours to pack up our belongings, and left our home on a flight to Florida. We were displaced for a few months. Life was upside down and I was unable to work because I didn't have reciprocity to practice therapy in another state. Many people left California at that time. I was granted a window of time in which I could take crisis calls from clients affected by the devastation from the earthquake, before Telehealth was a thing.

Fast forward to March 31st, our tenth wedding anniversary, that had originally been planned to be a huge celebration at our California home, with food, music, a DJ and dancing. Instead, living in Florida, my husband had to work late and the possessions of ours that made it to us, were packed floor to ceiling in boxes in a tiny apartment we rented. My mother had also hastily left her California home and went with us.

It was after 8 pm by the time we found a restaurant in which to eat dinner. We got back to the apartment, showered, and went to bed, only to be awakened around midnight by a raging fire that crackled loudly just outside of our front door. A car was in flames and my husband called 9-1-1. Realizing that the gas tank could explode at any moment, he herded us out the back, all of us running down the slope, as fast as our legs would carry us. I prayed and prayed for our safety and for life to settle. The police arrived in moments, put out the fire, and we returned to our apartment.

The next day, desiring some normalcy to everyday life, we decided that we needed to get the kids enrolled in pre-school and join the JCC (Jewish Community Center) to be connected to community. The JCC welcomed us and granted us access for free due to our circumstances. Accepting that kind gesture, I signed up for yoga and dance classes, while the children were well-cared for and having fun in their own part of the gym.

We all had been so overwhelmed and suffering from PTSD, due to the earthquake, that every time a big truck rumbled by we were throwing ourselves under a table or running to the nearest doorway for safety. A fun dance class was just what I needed to reduce stress.

I have danced since I was four and, for decades, performed professionally in several dance companies, but in this new environment, I chose to take my place at the back of the room.

In the row in front of me was a man, probably in his 60s, who was cheerfully taking on the challenge of the choreography and trying to keep up. I smiled to myself, thinking that he resembled my father, who would never be in a dance class. This man had the same swarthy, tan skin of my dad, a thin but strong build, and the thick, curly hair. My dad's hair had been dark but this man's hair was white.

Suddenly, he turned completely around to look directly into my eyes. My breath caught in my throat when I saw that he had the same crystal blue eyes as my dad. I instantly began to cry. He gently joked that I was not the first woman to cry when seeing his face. I stepped out of line and off to the side. He followed me, asking if I were okay. I told him that I was caught off guard because he looked so much like my father. The man was tender-hearted and kind and said that he would be honored to have such a lovely daughter.

I further explained that my dad had passed away 16 years prior and that I missed him. He extended his hand and gently shook mine, introducing himself. "I'm Leon," he said. I dissolved into a second round of sobs because my dad's name was Leo. Actually, his birth name was Leon. The building that housed his birth certificate had burned down and when he was issued a replacement certificate, he asked if he could change his name from Leon to Leo, the name he had always been called, and was given permission to do so.

I composed myself and we returned to the dance floor. We chatted again briefly, after class, and he offered a gentle hug, just like my dad's, before saying that he was just in town visiting friends and was leaving the next day. There was no doubt in my mind, that Dad was granted permission to inhabit Leon's physical body for another brief earthly hug.

I returned to the class a few more times but found myself feeling dizzy and nauseous while dancing. Three weeks later I discovered that on the night of our tenth anniversary, when the car flames were not the only flames ignited, that it resulted in my pregnancy with our third child. Sage was escorted here on the vibration of love and when Dad hugged me, she was wrapped in that hug as well.

VISITS FROM MY MOM

Blessedly, after Dad's passing, I got to have Mom close by in my life for the next 36 years. When she died, I thought I'd have regular visits from her but that hasn't been the case. She does, however, "wink" to us through faces in food.

When I was little, she used to create faces in the food she served me. My bologna sandwiches had mustard smiles, olives for eyes, and lettuce hair. Since her passing, I have saved so many photos of the face in the bell pepper on the grill and the clearly defined chocolate chip smiling face in the one cookie that ended up on the top of the pile of the 100 cookies I had baked for a school bake sale. There was the funny face that morphed from latte art that made us all laugh and the one in the bottom of the ice cream bowl. I imagine Mom smiling as she creatively sends them for us to discover.

She did "whisper" to me at one of the most important times. At 91, in a facility, and on her own terms, she let me know that it would be the last time that we would see her in this earthly body.

I had received a call from the facility while I was at my doctor's office, removing the compression bandages from my lumpectomy. Despite my disciplined and healthy lifestyle, the overwhelming stressors of the previous two years of my mom's decline had taken its toll on me.

The woman on the phone said that I needed to be there right away. Mom uncharacteristically had eaten a hearty lunch, even had seconds, and offered a sweeping wave to everyone in the room. She said, "Goodbye everyone! I'm done." Then, instead of attending the afternoon activity, she went to her bed to lie down. She wouldn't open her eyes or communicate further.

Right from the appointment, my husband drove me there to be with her. I rushed to her side and held her hand. She gently squeezed it, eyes still closed. I continued to talk softly to her. She didn't respond. I encouraged her to rest and get up for dinner when she was ready. She opened one eye, very briefly, to look at me. She winked and smiled but said nothing, and then closed her eye, expressionless, again.

We left after about 90 minutes and returned home so that I could rest and heal. I received another call at dinner time and then bedtime that Mom had not eaten or had water and had refused to communicate. All of her vitals were fine but she was still and not responding to others. They held the phone to her ear for me to speak with her but she didn't respond to me, either.

And so it went for the next three days. We visited her each day, which was a repeat of the first, without the hand squeezing, open eye, wink, or smile. Other family members accompanied us and held her hand, kissed her cheek, etc. She apparently was having painful muscle contractions, during which she made sounds but did not open her eyes or communicate. She pressed her lips together when they tried to hydrate her and had no food or water. Her previous instructions were clear that she didn't want IV fluids.

They were somber and told me that she would likely die within 48 hours. They said that without water, even athletes who are in excellent condition, can't survive more than five days. Mom, however, went eleven long days in this state.

The night before she passed, our whole family was visiting her, together, and I felt that same lifting off that I had felt with my father. I heard her say to me, while I watched her unmoving body, that this would be the last time that we would see her and to tell the others.

Each of us was experiencing our own grief about losing her. I gently told everyone what she had telepathically communicated to me. We all cried, held her and kissed her, rubbed her feet and caressed her hands as we simultaneously told her we couldn't bear to part from her but gave her permission to travel on her journey Home with G-d and the angels.

I remember watching my then, five-year-old grandson say goodbye to her. It cracked my heart in half. I didn't feel my body walk to the car that night. My husband drove but I don't recall the ride.

Storms rolled in during the night, with lots of thunder and lightning. Just after 4 a.m. I had the experience of gently being pulled up by my nightgown. It was as if someone were holding the fabric gathered at my heart and was lifting me to a sitting position. I opened my eyes and there was a bright light on the ceiling over my husband's side of the bed. I was fully awake and saw that his phone was lit up with a severe weather notification. Oh. I sighed, thinking that the light had been my mother. The phone screen went dark after a moment but the light remained. After the second notification, I got out of bed and moved my hand across the cell phone to break the beam and couldn't. I turned the phone upside down and the light continued to shine brightly.

I felt peaceful and calm. "Mom?" I asked aloud. The light moved to the corner of the room. I said, "Mom. I know that it's you. Thank you for coming here to say goodbye. I love you. Always and forever.

I send you off on words of love." I sat, barely breathing, as my husband and dog slept soundly through it all. "So grateful to have been your daughter. Thank you." It was an elevated sacred moment. At 4:45 a.m. the light darted across the ceiling and went out. I gasped and held my breath.

It thundered and I began to cry. I awakened my husband and he held me. Fifteen minutes later, at 5 a.m. the facility called to say that Mom had passed about fifteen minutes prior. A wail escaped my chest and throat that I didn't even recognize as coming from me. Our youngest daughter, the only one still living at home, as she was two weeks from high school graduation, came running into our room. The three of us held each other and wept.

Later in the day, the Hospice worker that was with my mother at the time of her passing, called with condolences and informed me that the Jewish funeral home had taken my mother, wearing only a shroud, and that we could come and collect her clothing and belongings at any time. She confirmed that my mother wore no jewelry or had any possessions on her person. When we initially moved Mom to the facility, we had taken her jewelry into safe-keeping at our home.

How odd it was, on the following day, when I received a phone call from the funeral director stating that my mother's watch was removed by them and placed in an envelope with my name on it to be picked up by me. I told him that it had been confirmed that my mother had no jewelry on her at the time of death. I asked if it could be a mistake. He asked me to describe the watch she may have worn. She had several watches but her favorite had been purchased when we took a trip to Hawaii and she traveled with us, 23 years prior. I assured him that I had all of her watches in my possession but I described that one to him. It was a gold watch with a white leather band that had cracks in it from years of wear. He stated that it was the very watch that he held in his hand.

I looked through her jewelry and was astonished that the watch was not there. I drove to the funeral home and he handed me the envelope containing the watch. I shook my head in disbelief, holding my mother's watch that radiated her energy. "How?" I asked. I heard my mom's voice say to me, "Thank you. I'm giving you your time back." I got chills on my whole body, which I view as confirmation from the Universe of truth.

I returned home to grieve and contact loved ones with the funeral arrangements, feeling as if Mom were right beside me. Jewish laws and customs have so much psychology and spirituality built into the rituals that I felt held in that sacred space throughout the couple of days it took while my relatives traveled to attend her funeral. I was numb and also present as I moved through the experience and continued to grieve at my own pace.

EXCERPT TO MY CHILDREN

You know that Nanny has come to me in dreams

that feel so real. Typically, dreams with her feel more like visitations. We are often doing something together and having a good time. I see the twinkle in her eyes with the endearing crinkles at the corners, see her smile, hear her Brooklyn accent, and her laughter. Just like in the foggy dream with my dad, I don't have the awareness that she's gone from this world until I awaken. It always feels so fulfilling to have spent time with her.

She, however, took a long time to visit. I'm sure that she's been busy helping others organize themselves and also sewing gowns for people on the other side, but I was hurt that she wasn't showing up. I reminded myself that earth-time and space-time are vastly different. I imagine I will also be very busy on the other side of the veil. Nothing is more important to me, though, than continuing to let you know that I love you, always and forever, and that I want you to live a life of enchantment.

I will do my best to "visit," if invited and allowed. Hopefully, I'll have accumulated lots of Brownie Points to be able to do this. I'll come to you in dreams if I can, and I'll also try to "borrow" kind, loving souls, with their consent of course, to look into your eyes and to hold you briefly. Naturally, I would never do anything to scare any of you.

If granted permission, I'll appear to you so realistically in dreams and visions that you will be sure that you are looking at me right in front of you and feeling my hugs in the flesh. Be on the lookout for synchronicities and inside jokes that no one else could know.

As you all know, I will send you hearts. In all forms. Whether they're leaves or rocks, or even clouds, with the help of the angels, they will all be from me. They're intended to be touchstones, not sources of pain from separation.

Maybe you'd like to compile photos with the hearts I will send. Feel free to collect my photos of the faces in the food from Nanny and put them into a family album to hand down through the generations.

It has been such an honor to be your mother, and *Savta* (grandmother in Hebrew) to your children.

All of the stories remind you that I do believe in reincarnation, G-d's plan and our own soul's free will, and that angels are among us, always, helping us to navigate through life.

I have witnessed, and believe, all of the subjective evidence that souls, in concert with G-d and the angels, orchestrate their own passing. I've counseled so many people who have talked about sitting a vigil with their loved one for days, or even weeks, and during that one hour that they went home from the hospital to shower and get fresh clothes, their loved one slipped away from life. In other families, once everyone was present, the soul departed. I do believe that the events unfold exactly as they are intended, for the Highest learning or experience of all concerned.

Our Jewish teachings say that we honor our dead by valuing life and living our lives to the fullest. I would never want you to give up the pursuit of happiness and joy just because I was not physically walking beside you.

CHAPTER TEN: TO YOUR CHILDREN

This section might include your children, stepchildren, grandchildren, or loved ones who have felt as if they became your children or grandchildren. Consider whether or not you want to address them all together or each one, separately. Tell them what they mean to you, what qualities you admire about them (even if you've been at odds,) and what you want them to know. Even if it is out of character for you, I urge you, again, to be thoughtful and sensitive, while being honest. If you've always been a jokester, you can still express yourself in your authentic voice, but maybe also allow a tenderness to be detected in your Instructions.

An excerpt to my children follows, with one of my pieces of poetry:

EXCERPT TO MY CHILDREN

Remember the piece I wrote titled: *How To Live When You're Away From Me?* It's a good time to remind you of that. It applies to all of you, still, and to your children as well, so I'm giving you a copy of it.

How to Live When You Are Away from Me
By Terry Segal

Don't be careless with my life that you live. Wear light colors after dark. Don't run with scissors or a lollipop in your mouth. Balloons are the number one choking hazard for children under the age of five. If you're hiking, don't put a plastic bag on your head.

Don't talk while you're chewing, you could choke. Put the stick down, you could take someone's eye out with that. Even if the lodge is too cold, never put a space heater in your bath water.

Don't drink and drive. As a matter of fact, don't drink at all. Don't jump up and down after you eat, you could throw up. In case you should suddenly decide to wear them, buy flame-resistant, not just flame-retardant, pajamas. Don't step on a crack; your mother has enough going on. Don't take the tags off of any pillows. Hold the blade away from you while cutting your bagel. If you get caught in an undertow, remember to swim parallel to the shore and that moss grows on the north side of the trees. Make sure the trail back to my heart is clear, but don't leave breadcrumbs. Birds eat them. Don't ever barbeque your friend's Christmas tree to get rid of it, with or without the tinsel. Brush your teeth before you go to bed. Don't say anything you wouldn't want printed on the front page of the newspaper.
Say your prayers. I'll be saying mine.

Don't tax your Guardian Angel. Look behind the door for instructions, even if you won't read them. Bring your seat back to an upright position with tray table securely fastened. Keep your eyes on the road and both hands on the wheel. Buckle your seat belt. Carry traveler's checks, even if you've never heard of them.

Don't talk to strangers or take any wooden nickels.

If you have a splinter, paint it with rubber cement and when it dries, peel it off. For healing boo-boos, blow on them and then kiss them.
Don't play with matches or snakes.
Don't try to keep your eyes open when you sneeze.
Bundle up, snuggle in, and know that I love you.

THINGS THAT DELIGHT ME

In this section, I invite you to list all of the things that have delighted you. It can be things from a long time ago. Maybe you have pushed them to the back burner and it would be good for you to remember them for yourself. As for others, the list might be a way to remember and celebrate you. It might also offer a way for your loved ones to honor you or participate in an activity or event that may evoke fond memories in them or introduce them to a sport or experience they have not tried before.

There's no right or wrong way to do this so just have at it. Step into the stream of consciousness and start where you start and end where you end. Undoubtedly, once the juices are flowing, you'll continue to think of things to add on to this list.

EXCERPT TO MY FAMILY: (for space purposes here I wrote in lines but suggest a vertical list. Use as many columns as you need.)

Love, of course my family, children, puppies, laughing, nature, trees, flowers, birds, butterflies, my gardens of herbs, vegetables, flowers, change of seasons, seasonal tablescapes, art, glitter, colored pencils, markers, crayons, watercolor paint, rubber stamps, writing, angels, good books, fairies, our tea and chocolate room, teapots, teacups, tea, "little food," Medieval castles, rooms and parties with themes, enchanted woodland scenes, aprons, sandalwood incense, candles, gazing ball, ice cream, organic hotdogs, grilled vegetable sandwiches, huge salads, the beach, make-up, watching Hunter play baseball, Jordan's Nest Cafes, watching movies with Daddy and also the family, Downton Abbey, England, picnics, photos of the French, English, and Italian countryside, Sage's playing the violin, Native American drumming and flute music, Adrian Von Zeigler music, Celtic music, fire pits, S'mores, the moon, stars, astrology, Sascha's silent laughter, hearts, helping others, and Judaism.

I have many specific and personal things to say to each of my children. I strongly suggest that you address each of yours in some way that is personalized. It's important for each one to feel seen and heard as individuals. Even if a relationship has been rocky, hearing you say or write something that is loving or complimentary or a quality that you recognize and admire in them can change lives.

CHAPTER ELEVEN:
YOUR LEGACY STATEMENT

We are guided throughout our lives by specific statements or teachings that special people, such as our parents, teachers, and other loved ones, have spoken to us. They carry an energy that is eternal. My dad's legacy statement was, "Your word is your bond." He used to also say, often, "Never let the sun set on your anger," and "It's as important to be beautiful on the inside as the outside." My mom's was, "You don't know what you can do until you try." Mine is, "Life is a journey. Make it enchanting."

I wish to leave the legacy of love and the framework of my life's work that includes the Ten Enchanted Keys for living a life that is as Happily Ever After as possible. That is included in my book, *The Enchanted Journey: Finding the Key That Unlocks You*. I'd like each of you to have your own virtual keyring with the keys on it that you carry in your heart and mind at all times. I believe that following the principles of each key can alter the perception of the whole Universe. Here they are:

Mindfulness

Mindfulness is awareness in the present moment. Being where you are, right now, noticing breath, tension, physical sensations, thoughts and emotions. Observing them with neutrality or love, but without judgment.

Altered Perceptions

Flipping the way you view things from your style,

work, relationships and what matters to you. Being open-minded as you consider energy that "is," without putting it in the categories of "good" and "bad." Things are not always as they seem. "Bad" things may bring you insight and allow you to create change. "Good" things may have been good at one point but no longer serve you.

Journaling

Journaling is a writing meditation. It's a rest stop in which to dream, flow, and express yourself. Art journals do the same with images, color, and composition. Some journaling combines both imagery and words.

Sensory Experiences

This Key unlocks the sights, sounds, smells, tastes and textures along the path. It's a journey through the senses that add sparkle to life's experiences and deepen the memory of them.

Reduced Clutter

Clutter can exist on the physical, mental, emotional, and spiritual planes. When you de-clutter your life, you make room for new possibilities. "Marie Kondo" your life, only keeping what you love and what serves a purpose, on all of the planes.

Humor

Laughter is good medicine. Get in touch with what makes you laugh, when you laugh, and how you can laugh more often. Laughing "with," instead of "at," is key.

Movement

Movement recharges your battery, enhances productivity, relieves stress from your mind and body, increases flexibility, and aids your organs in functioning at their best.

Art
Play with shapes, colors, textures, and images to express yourself without a single word, if you wish. When your physical body is no longer the container for everything, the page can be filled. There are no "mistakes," only learning.

Nature
Realign yourself with the beauty, serenity, and healing of the natural world. The term, forest bathing, comes from the Japanese phrase, *shinrin-yoku,* coined in 1982, by Tomohide Akiyama. The healing benefits of unplugging from technology and the stress of everyday life by returning to the woods, are well documented. There's reverence in the sanctuary of the forest or at the base of a tree in your own backyard.

Meditation
A rest stop in life to relax, restore, regenerate and revive your tired spirit. The benefits are great and you need not sit in pretzel pose. Meditations can be experienced while sitting, writing, walking, dancing, painting, chanting, drumming, and all while breathing.

* * *

During the writing of this, while I was looking up something else completely unrelated, my computer, as they are want to do, redirected me to a story about John Schneider. He's the actor/country singer best known for his role as Bo Duke in the 1980s TV show, *The Dukes of Hazzard*. I almost clicked out of it but saw that it involved a message received from the beyond.

The story was about the Schneiders "failed marriage" of 21-years and his second-chance at love, with actress/producer/make-up artist, Alicia Allain. They had been working together and were inseparable since 2015. They married in 2019. Shortly after, she had been diagnosed with Her2 breast cancer and he became her partner in health. After they devoted themselves to changes in diet, lifestyle, and religious/spiritual faith-based prayer, Allain was deemed cancer-free. Sadly, however, she died unexpectedly in February of 2023, with no cause of death listed. She was 53 years old. Schneider, 63, who referred to his wife as his "beautiful Smile," said, "My beautiful Smile is pain free, living in her new body alongside Jesus." Her obituary reads, "In lieu of flowers, please say prayers for her surviving family, tell someone you love that you love them in her honor, hug them and hold them tight."

Devastated beyond description, Schneider was with a friend who asked him what Alicia would say to him, if she were able to send him a message. Schneider immediately said it would be, "Make me proud." Feeling the power in that, he wrote it on Post-It notes and has incorporated it into several aspects of his life.

Think about what message you'd like to leave behind to your loved ones or the world. Maybe it's even one you'd want engraved on your headstone.

This "accidental" stumbling upon this story touched my heart and confirmed that, across religions and worlds, there is a universal connection to life, love, and death.

A story arrived in my Inbox about another lovely woman with a bright smile, who was vibrant and full of life, yet also dying. Her name was Louise Shockey. I had been praying for her for over a year and a half since I learned of her advanced cancer diagnosis.

I know of her because my son-in-law is a hunter, as is Louise's famous husband, Jim Shockey, and their daughter, Eva Shockey. Jim Shockey is a professional hunter, an award-winning outdoor television writer and producer, wildlife photographer, videographer, naturalist, wilderness guide and outfitter. Eva, having grown up with both of them, is all about family, the outdoors, hunting and living a balanced, healthy lifestyle.

A photo was posted of Louise, smiling her radiant smile in the face of death. Over a year and a half earlier, she was given only a few short months to live. She had fought hard and valiantly and, at the end, Jim posted her picture and wrote: "Her strength defies the illness as her spirit strengthens and her body surrenders."

They shared the journey publicly and were amazed by the outpouring of love from all of us, strangers, who prayed for her and the family throughout her struggle. Louise inspired everyone to love fully and deeply until those last breaths and perhaps even beyond. She was an important link in that chain of love.

A parallel traditional Jewish teaching is that we stand on the shoulders of those who came before us. We have a responsibility to live life in such a way as to make our ancestors and future generations proud. The synchronicity of finding Alicia's and Louise's messages did not go unnoticed. An encouraging message left behind can uplift and guide loved ones who are struggling emotionally.

I mindfully try to live the way of my ancestors and I hope that my children will continue to share our ancestral beliefs with their own children, grandchildren, and great-grandchildren.

There is deep reverence for all customs of death and dying. At my mother's funeral, Sascha, our eldest daughter, read this Cherokee poem:

> When you were born,
> you cried and the world rejoiced.
> Live your life in such a way
> that when you die,
> the world cries
> and you rejoice.

Sit quietly, perhaps in nature, and think about the legacy statement or message you'd like to leave behind for others to hold on to when they're feeling unsteady. Likely, your loved ones will be able to hear your voice speaking those words and also feel inspired.

CHAPTER TWELVE:
YOUR WORLDLY POSSESSIONS

Major worldly possessions like homes, cars, and boats are covered in the Will, but what about your computer passwords, keys, places where money is stashed, (think mattresses, between the pages of a certain book and/or Swiss bank accounts,) journals, collections, costume jewelry and memory cards from your camera? Who would you want to be in charge of those things? It might be a different person than the one you've assigned as your Executor. The Executor you have chosen may be great with the distribution of finances, possessions, and accepting the organized responsibility of the role. Another person may be better suited to carrying out your wishes about where your family photo albums should go and who gets your cookware. Some decisions are made with the mental realm, like financial ones, which create more emotional riffs than one might imagine, and other decisions are best carried out by someone who can move about more comfortably in the emotional world.

You might begin with the monetary responsibilities and move to the emotionally-based ones. Not that money isn't an emotional issue. A whopping 70% of families get into disputes over inheritance issues. According to estate planning specialists, communication is the key to your best shot at keeping this from happening with your loved ones. There are no guarantees but it's advised that the family members are all brought into the conversation early on, about who will get what and why, so there are no "surprises." If there are hurt feelings, they can be worked through while there is still opportunity. Another plus to discussing things in advance.

There are instances that I'm aware of that make discussing things in advance an unacceptable choice for some. One case involved a dad who didn't want his children to know of his financial wealth. His wife/their mother, was deceased and had known he was wealthy but they didn't live that lifestyle and agreed to raise their children without knowledge of that. They believed in hard work for everyone and he thought that revealing his net worth would negatively impact his children, even when they were adults.

He sought therapy to discuss the issue of whether or not they might feel betrayed by him for withholding the money while they had struggled to find their niches and success in the world. He wanted his "good surprise" of wealth at his passing to be a gift to them all.

This man had gotten the idea from an article he read that had impacted him. It was about a father who had secretly told each of his children that he or she was his favorite and never to tell the others. Then, at the reading of the Will, they were all informed of that. This man had decided to do that with his own children and wondered if he should tell them when they were all gathered together for a holiday, rather than letting them find out posthumously. I believe that these are very thoughtful and important topics of discussion.

No matter how old adult children are, they all want to have felt loved and special in the eyes of their parents. Childhood wounds, or their *perceived* wounds, may or may not be healed. Are you old enough to remember the Smothers Brothers? Tom and Dick Smothers would get into it with the phrase, "Mom always liked you best!" That's why it's important for you to consider what you know, or think you know, about your loved ones. As mentioned earlier, certain people are going to be better with the cut-and-dry aspects, while others are not.

Think about how each of them experience loss and grief and see if you have some specific suggestions for their individualized personalities. Consider the gifts that will be most meaningful and who might be best suited to perform the various tasks.

For instance, one person charged with the task to go through clothing might touch each item, moved by the memory of Mom's well-loved dress, special-occasion earrings, or the tie Dad wore at their wedding. Another person might just scoop it all up and stuff it into trash bags to take to Goodwill. Who decides what the survivors need? Someone who can get the task done who isn't so sentimental or someone who will be trusted to consider each item and hold on to a few that have special meaning? It's going to be different for every family. My Instructions would state that each member must voice his or her opinion to the group and the group must come to a compromise that considers everyone's feelings and situation. I'd never feel okay about someone being left out or having his or her wishes completely ignored.

Some things cannot and do not need to be discussed in advance, but what can help is an agreement to discuss every action that will be taken, afterward, maybe with a chosen mediator for disagreements. It can be a beloved friend of the family or another relative or an unbiased therapist. This seems to be the best way to handle this particular kind of strife.

In my family, my mother became the guardian of her parents' possessions, and my father's as well, after his passing. Then, this was all handed down to me. I treasure my father's mezuzah on his necklace but I don't wear it. I have his dog tags from when he was a Sergeant in the U.S. Army. My grandmother's aforementioned Cameo, that she used to carefully pin to her dress, forever holds the memory of her sweet spirit and milky soft skin that resembled the ivory of the face on the Cameo woman, herself. My grandfather was given a medal for his oration of McKinley's Dead, when he was 13, following the assassinnation of our 25th President, William McKinley. I also have his prized pocket watch. My mother was my troop's Girl Scout Leader and I cherish her pins and my sashes on which Mom had hand-sewed each badge. But what will I do with all of those things? I'll probably put it all into one large sealed bin and hand it down to our youngest daughter, Sage. And why her? Because she cherishes relics from the past and has a sentimental heart. My eldest daughter also has a soft spot in her heart for memories, but keeps a "clutter-free" home, as does my son. People and memories are meaningful to them, but they choose not to have the material possessions to remind them of their experiences.

COLLECTIONS

This deserves a special section because people who are collectors of things have put a lot of passion, love, time, energy and money into collecting things that were important to them. Sometimes it's a matter of "one man's trash is another man's treasure," and in other instances, collections may have a significant monetary value.

I fondly remember a dear client who came to me after having been given a formidable diagnosis. She pondered the statement of her doctors to "go home and get your life in order." She began by saying that she was never a person of order. Rather, she called herself a person of whimsy who loved to travel, planning spontaneous and adventurous trips. She was an artist and a devoted animal advocate. She also loved the old Hollywood movies and had special bookshelves built to house all the ones she owned. Over the months, we talked about what matters at the end of a life, her life specifically, and it came down to the people and the relationships that she had fostered. But what about her collections? She had two very large collections of things that she stated "assumed" would be taken over by her children. I listened to her reasoning about why she kept putting off the discussion with them, week after week, that I urged her to have. She finally said that she knows they will want to live in that house forever and would be thrilled to take over the curation of her collections as they always enjoyed it too. She didn't want to be "morbid" in discussing it.

I think to appease me, she finally had the discussion with them. She said she did it to come in and say, "See? I told you so." But what she learned, shocked her. We spent several sessions discussing the heartbreak she felt when her adult children told her that neither of them had any interest in or wanted anything to do with her collections and had always been afraid to have to deal with the burden of them once she was gone. They were trying to be kind but direct in telling her that neither of them wanted to live in their childhood house and didn't want the responsibility of renting it, either.

She was angry, hurt, and sad but came to terms with what they had shared and moved through her grief into action. Many discussions were had after that and they helped her by clearing out all of their own possessions that they didn't want or need from the house. She researched organizations that were interested in accepting her collections and had been in the process of having them come to take them when her health took a turn for the worse.

Relatives who lived nearby were put in charge of selling the house, which they did when she died. It was very sad, but so important that she had the courage to talk to her children and find out how they truly felt, before her passing.

My mother collected clowns. She was an administrative assistant to a Junior High School principal for years and many people gifted her with clowns. I was left with her beloved clown collection. The only problem is that I absolutely hate clowns. Hate them. My children hate them as well. They always viewed them as creepy and scary. My sentiments exactly. But out of great respect for my mother's love of them, I tried to find them a home in which a person or organization might take all of them. I had even painted pictures of clowns and gifted them to her for various occasions. I didn't even want those back. A family friend happily took those but after almost five years of the rest of them living in a big box in the otherwise empty and neat garage, I had to move them out. I'd had no takers from marketplace ads and eventually I had to bless them away to the community charity in our area. I felt awful but I had made a valiant effort prior to letting them go in that way.

I never set out to be a collector of anything but, as it turns out, I have quite a large rubber stamp collection that grew when my mom's collection was inherited. We used to love to go to rubber stamp shows and watch demos on the latest techniques for embossing an image, shading, coloring, using a stamp mask to do overlays, etc. Each month we'd have an art date and make all of the cards for the month ahead to send out for birthdays, anniversaries, etc. Those stamps still represent years of fun that we had together. I cherish them. Some of the stamps did not reflect my taste and I allowed myself to give them to others who wanted them or to use them for art projects with the grandchildren.

I've also collected teapots, without intending to do so. I cherish them as well and they are on display and for use in our tea and chocolate room in our home.

I'm a prolific artist and writer and my Instructions include the suggestion to keep my journals (my *many, many* journals!) There is a disclaimer that reads: If anything is contained in my lifetime of journals that has you questioning if I were any different than you knew me to be, dismiss it. We all ponder possibilities, we vent from our personality selves, and most musings are not from our Highest selves. Just consider that all people are whole in our expressions, our wounds and broken places, as well as our dreams and aspirations. Everything else is the in-between of life's experiences and what we did with that precious lifetime.

I make so much art, as well, which is an expression of my very soul. The books I have written, my poetry, my unwritten manuscripts — I don't expect my loved ones to finish anything I've started but I ask them to please be the guardian of it all. And by "them," you already know that I mean Sage. My jewelry, my recipes, and all things enchanted. All of those items tell the stories. Enjoy the precious photos that capture snippets of my life well-lived. Most important to me is the remembrance of my love of our precious family, forever, so that future generations may feel it.

So please think about your possessions and your collections and talk to your loved ones about them. May you find peace in what you'd like to do about those things that have mattered to you. You've put your time, energy, money, and passion into them and so deserve to feel like you have the power to express what will become of them.

Discuss your Will and division of property while you can mediate and repair hurt feelings, if there are any, instead of sealing them in perpetuity. Avoid conflicts in the future. People assign meaning, such as, "This was left to YOU?" That confirms that Dad loved you more…Who gets the writing desk? If this child gets that, what would be meaningful to have instead? How would you expect to make these decisions, while you're here? How do you want to handle the emotions and process of deciding?

I encourage you to make decisions, put your plans into action, discuss it with your loved ones and then live your best life.

CHAPTER THIRTEEN: FINAL THOUGHTS

In this excerpt from Merrit Malloy's poem, ***Epitaph,*** she wrote,
"Love doesn't die,
People do.
So, when all that's left of me
Is love,
Give me away."

I'd like to include another of my poems here, to be read at my funeral, where I invite those present to listen to it with their hearts as they hear me speak to them from mine.

You all have my permission if you'd like it to be read at yours.

When Time Has Run Out
By Terry Segal

Weep not for my passing,
Rather, celebrate my life.
As I morph into another form,
Know that I am with you, still.

That it is not the air,
But I, who wipe your tears dry.
I walk beside you
And move in and out of your thoughts.

I am a fragrance, wafting through your senses,
That bookmarks volumes
Of our time shared.

Hold the memory of my laughter in your heart
And play it often.
Feel the flesh and breath and joy of my love.

Tell the stories of my life.
All of them.
Not just the ones in which I was saintly.
All of them.
So that I may be remembered whole.

For that is who I was when I walked upon this earth.
Who you knew me to be.
One who was honored to have known you.
One who was blessed to have known love.

I love you.
Always and forever.
THE END
(but never the end…)

ACKNOWLEDGMENTS

As always, I'd like to thank my dear family for their unwavering love and support in everything I do. To Fred, my husband and best friend, whom I will love across all Universes and throughout eternity, thank you for coming in to check on me each time you heard me crying and for tiptoeing out when you realized it was because I was writing this book.

Sascha, Jordan, and Sage, you are my most precious gifts. I thank you for taking the time to read this book, which I know was a very difficult topic for you. Sascha, you were the most resistant because, whenever I talked about it, you'd cover your ears and sing over me. Each of you has provided valuable feedback to my process.

Your dear children, my grandchildren, are a constant source of comic relief, innocence, purity and love that this world so sorely needs. I'm grateful to have you all so close.

Gratitude to Lee Clevenger, for having a tender heart and such enthusiasm for my writing. Having your guidance along the way has been deeply appreciated.

A big hug of thanks to George Weinstein, whose wisdom of this writing world has no bounds.

To my gentle readers, I thank you from the bottom of my heart. You're listed in alphabetical order because I could never list you in order of my love for you. Some of you shared the broad impact of the book, while others dug into the depths of word choices. All of you made it better. You are: H. W. "Buzz" Bernard, Paul A. Bussard, Lee Clevenger, Monika S. Eichler, Sharon Levine Khoury, Dr. Susan Russell, Jordan Segal, Sage Segal, Sascha Segal, and Cathy Askowitz Tesserot.

As always, I'm grateful to the angels, those seen and unseen, for offering love and guidance, daily.